M000012276

MELISSA PROPHET'S

MELISSA PROPHET

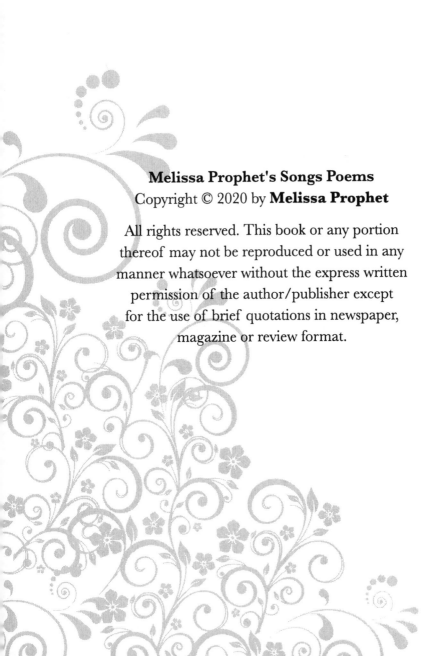

Melissa Prophet's Songs Poems
Copyright © 2020 by **Melissa Prophet**

MELISSA PROPHET'S

Songs Poems

Dedication

I want to dedicate this book to my Mom Barbara Jean Prophet who went home to be with Lord on July 6, 1990 and my Grandmother Bonnie Ruth Prophet who went home to be with the Lord on June 7, 2020. When people say to me you are such a blessing I always reply, "I get that from my Mothers". Each had a heart of gold, extremely compassionate and a sense of humor that would always light up the room with laughter. To my children Tiffany, Malaysia, Elijah, Isaiah and Brendan and Grandchildren Jasmine, Janyia, Jayla and Mya for teaching me how to be the best version of myself. I would also like to thank my sisters Theresa and Tamara for being awesome Aunt's that always go above and beyond for their nieces and nephews. My Best friends Carmen Wesley and Nickola Sybblis, Tonia Phillips for always pushing to me to be my best. My mate Walter D. Watkins for being an awesome supporter of myself and our children there is nothing you will not do for our family and I greatly appreciate you for that. I would like to thank Rhonda Gilbert for inspiring me to publish my book after I read her book "It's All About Perception" here is one of my favorite quotes from her book for Day 39 "The caterpillar does not have to wait to become a butterfly to start seeing himself as one." Also to my niece Shellis and Aunt Gloria you both are amazing and after receiving your Donor Transplants the doctors stated it's a miracle that you both survived, "GOD HAS THE FINAL SAY!!"

Table of Contents

Lost Man

My brother, we don't need your DISRESPECT, nor your NEGLECT, we need your RESPECT.

Look around, you're the reason why so many of our children run astray, because it's so easy for you to walk away.

How can it be that you quote yourselves as kings past looking at the future it no wonder that didn't last.

The majority of you demonstrate no love, no respect, no family values, no spiritual values, NO, NO, NO, NOTHING.

I'm a PIMP! Is that rewarding? No, it SICKENING!

If we were the Queens and King of the past. Why can't that clearly been seen through your actions?

It's time to STOP teaching the children division, and we CHALLENGE you to start making wiser decisions.

The product of such is WE.

Mama's crying because she's trying to fill a role that she NEVER should be applying for (filling your shoes).

She closes her hearts door to feel nothing no more.

It's no wonder that she chooses to ignore, the man that's offering her more, because your actions have made her heart too sore to explore LOVE anymore.

And in loves absence CANCER starts to explore.

Lost Man PLEASE find yourself so the FAMILY and
COMMUNITY can start healing and the DEVIL can STOP
STEALING our JOY.

I thought You were the One I Could Learn to Trust

I thought you were the one I could learn
to trust

But you're like them ALL so full of lust

What did I do to deserve you

I've been honest from the beginning and it
was easy to

I took you among my friends and you
tried to begin

Another relationship right under
my nose

I guess I'm the Weed and
she's the Rose

All my (so called) friends
and family knew and
didn't say a word

I guess they're the same as you

But I'm different BECAUSE I WOULD NEVER DO THAT TO YOU NEVER!!!

I would never intentionally hurt anyone, for any reason

But I'm surrounded by girls that are like Vultures and I'm the meat

Or surrounded by little boys so full of heat

Maybe God

Maybe God wanted us to be able to tell
each other apart?

Made one race light and the other
one dark.

Maybe didn't think we'd get caught up in
that part?

Thought we'd deal with each other like we
have a HEART?

Maybe thought we'd be able to
come up with a solution without
it resulting in a revolution?

Thought we'd maybe be
able to treat each other fairly
without referring back to the
constitution?

Why did we forget to deal with each other like we have a HEART?

Maybe God truly wants us to remember that part.

Friend or Foe?

Are you a friend or foe?

I thought I knew, but now I just don't know.

If actions, speak louder than words.

Then what are you saying to me?

I've been wondering is the friendship an illusion not all that it's cracked up to be.

I've been a true blue did whatever you asked me to gladly.

Are you a friend or foe?

If actions speaks louder than words, I guess I already know.

Leo

In him I see the radiance and aura of a king.

In his presence I feel like a blessed queen.

His eyes reveal the depth of a gentle soul.

In his arms I feel as if I'm engulfed in
a goosedown comforter being protected
from the bitter freezing cold.

He has the walk of a proud graceful lion and
the agility of an eagle flying.

His voice graces my ears like a
perfect summer gentle breeze.

I wish he were mine so that I
could appreciate his presence
all the time.

In the Absence of the King

In the absence of the king the kingdom runs wild

Now there's one less man for every woman
and child

The queen awaits for the kings return

While the princess and the prince are
unsure of what went wrong

And the feelings burns

Were they not worthy enough is what
they wondered in the meantime

Did they do something so wrong
that made the king want to
resign

As the years roll by they
realized that the king was no
more than a peasant

Never cared enough to make a call or send a present

Now sitting next to the queen is a new king

It's kinda funny because at the wedding of the
queen and the old king he carried the ring

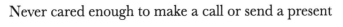

Now 15 years later in walks the king, but
now he rules nothing

It took the price and the princess to
realize after all of these years

It wasn't them that did something,

It was the king that did nothing

Smoke Robinson Concert

You played and I stayed.

You took and I gave.

I gave and you took.

I chose to get to know you because I didn't want to judge the cover of your book.

My head was telling me to run while my heart was telling me to stay.

Funny how the devil loves it that way.

Now I can see you for who you truly are, my head is telling me to leave and my heart isn't much far-and I know you feel the same, you started the games

Tired of fighting, tired of not trusting, tired of dealing with a man that bases his emotions off lusting.

Time invested, but not wasted. The lesson I learned is what I'll hold onto, that is what I was trying to explain to you.

I made love to you from my soul, because at the time it's what I thought you were giving me. Thought you'd teach me something different and assist me in not repeating history.

I'm trying to elevate, this you can't see?

Didn't think that you would just play with me, this whole experience has been crazy.

Or am I?

Keep pimping, keep flirting, keep doing what you do!

Just don't get mad whenever your mate starts doing it to.

Another relationship ends so another one can begin.

When does it end, starting new relationships over, and over, and over and over again?

Hello my name is Joe Some and I would like to take you and your family out to dinner. How many times have you used that line?

18

I Have Issues

Someone told me because he was offended by a poem I wrote titled Lost Man that, "I Have Issues".

Well I respond, "My issue is you!"

How shall I begin with my issues?

I am a woman trying to survive in a world that constantly feeds me lies, about my lips, my skin tone, etc. BUT the worse lie came from you, the so called King that thinks he's most HIGH.

The lies that you told me to get between my thighs.

How was I to know that you had a wife. I asked you once, guess I should have asked twice. Your lie. But I have issues.

How did I know that I was making her cry and wondering why hubby wasn't at home on time. Because you were FEEDING me lies, and at the same time, being the DEMISE of the family unit which I cherish so MUCH!

But I have issues.

Oh, I have A issue! My issue is YOU and as I contemplate what to do, although by now I care, I WALK away from you.

You were my issue, I hope the next female sees through.

So that you won't become her issue too.

Change is Strange

First it's love than it's pain

It use to be so easy but now it's a constant strain

Change is strange

There was a time when you used to spend all of your dimes

To keep me on the line

Now I guess your thoughts are who has time

Change is strange

There was a time when I knew you had my back 100%

Now I'm listening to 50 cents

Now I'm being published for your past pains, that treated you strange

Or are you hiding something and you believe
I'm doing the same?

You've become so inconsistent, when you use to be so persistent
about this partnership

Change is strange especially when the
other person's feelings haven't changed

Another chapter closed for a new one to
start all over again

Next time maybe the issues won't remain
the same

Hopefully honestly will at least
remain

So we won't have to change
partners again, and again, and
again, and again

When does it end?

Made in the USA
Middletown, DE
26 April 2022

64760528R00020